POETRY IS A PUZZLE

Acknowledgments:

Poetry transports me to another place, where I can cause a blank sheet of paper to come alive as I put thought into words. I would like to thank The Oasis poetry class for making those words sing with their helpful suggestions and their unbiased encouragement.

Previously Published Poems:

International Library of Poetry
From a Safe Place – 2002
Mirror, Mirror – 2002
Christmas Interrupted – 2003
The Collector – 2003
Listen – 2005
Insomnia – 2007

Oasis Journal
Witch Creek – 2009
Special Delivery – 2010
Fait Accompli – 2011
Last Dance – 2013
Smoke Rings – 2014
Insomnia – 2015
Welcome to Paris – 2016

San Diego Poetry Annual
Christmas Interrupted – 2016

POETRY IS A PUZZLE

POEMS

MARILYN L. KISH MASON

BLUE VORTEX PUBLISHERS

POETRY IS A PUZZLE

First Edition
ISBN-13: 978-0972621069
ISBN-10: 0-972621067

First paperback printing, July, 2018
Printed in the United States of America
The text in this book is composed in Palatino Linotype

Cover photo by my father, Raymond E. Kish Sr.

BLUE VORTEX PUBLISHERS

Poetry is a Puzzle

Thoughts scatter
blown like leaves
in the wind,
words emerge
then fade.
I reach for a dream,
catch merely the tail.
Mysteries of love,
ambiguities of future,
blurred memories
of the past,
all part of a picture
that becomes clear
only if the pieces
finally align.

Table of Contents

Country

I farm a little plot of things to say,
with not much frontage on the busy road

~ Ted Kooser

Country Comfort

Lost in my Latte,
I shun city crowds,
flee to country calm,
blot out the thrum
of tedious traffic flow.
Here, neon lights
do not disguise the vast
display of starry nights,
or arc of meteor flights.

Dawn, a cock crows
his opening solo
on a narrow rail,
his notes converge
with a cacophony
of clucking hens,
as barnyard beasts
converse in
foreign tongues.

In four-leaf clover bliss
kissed by summer's
golden sun,
I drink the milk
of creature kindness.
Nourished by this
delicious daydream,
I return to mingle
with my urban flock.

Prairie Farm
(Final Harvest)

Cock and hen,
feathers ruffled
danced a fandango
as an indifferent brood
pecked the ground ingesting
pebbles into their gizzards.

Playful pups
chased feral cats
around the farm yard,
distracting them from
duties in the barn.

Bossy, Bessie and Fern
head-locked in stanchions,
flicked fly swatter tails
shoo away tormentors'
biting their dappled rumps.

Combines lumbered
through fields
like prehistoric mammoths,
steel teeth gnashing through
golden seas of wheat...

Now dust devils
twist in the wind
like crazed exclamation points,
suck up earth, fling debris
into barren furrows.

A leaning, gap-toothed fence
surrounds a decrepit barn.
The haymow agape,
gasps a final breath
before walls implode.

A white vee points south,
as geese begin their autumn
migration to warmer climes,
the farmers' follow,
leaving hope behind.

All cry out as they fly away.
Only the geese will return.

Smoke Rings

Pungent odor of tobacco smoke
clings to curtains, clothes, a white cloud
encircles my father's head as he lights
another cigarette off the one before.
I empty ashtrays full of malignant ashes.

Father wears bib overalls
with many pockets. One pocket stashes
a tobacco pouch with drawstring and tab.
He fills his pouch from a Union Jack,
or a Prince Albert tobacco tin.

Another pocket contains papers for
rolling, deftly balancing thin tissue
between his fingers he shakes tobacco
along the paper, rolls it, seals it with spit
then twists the ends.

He carries matches in a third pocket.
Removing a match from the box,
strikes the head along the rough leg
of his overalls, it flares and the acrid
odor of sulfur assaults the senses.

Nocturnal phone calls begin in my twenties.
A heart attack first, by now he has opted
for readymade unfiltered Phillip Morris.
More attacks follow, pneumonia, cancer,
emphysema, he smokes until the end.

My father is my hero, my loss profound.
Like diffusing smoke rings, he drifts away.

Often I think back to the country life that shaped me;
taught me the miracles of natures seasons

~ Marilyn L. Kish Mason

Summer

Cock crows
sun shows
sleepy face
songbirds wake
serenade from
feathered nests
sheltered arms
leafy trees
cows low
udders fill
with new milk
rich and sweet
barn cats lick
whiskers wet
farmer's treats
from squirting teats
day evolves
revolves around
ripened crops
corn and wheat
needing water
weeding reaping
seasons change
retreat repeat

it is summer
everything grows
until it snows

Ghosts on the Prairie

Weary winds whisper
through abandoned farms.
Owls hoot in empty barn lofts
as the ululations of coyotes
carry over canyon ridges.

The echo of harmonicas
wail near a cold campfire.
Twigs snap eerily
behind mesquite bushes.
Scudding clouds veil
the Hunter's Moon,
as claps of thunder
drum in the distance.

These sights and sounds
of the prairie are recalled
along crisscrossed ruts
of wagon wheels, horses hooves.
Trails rife with arrowheads,
parched buffalo bones,
and make-shift crosses
where buzzards perch.

Swirling dust devils
tumble thistledown
across the expanse
of time and destiny,
chasing prairie ghosts.

Humor

Be yourself: everyone else is already taken

~ Oscar Wilde

Pass the Cheese Please

As for me...

skip the Brie

What's with the Swiss

a holey miss

leave Provolone

completely alone

Limburger smells

truly repels

let's talk Feta

it's much betta

nothing could be sweeta

than good old Velveeta

Daily Grind
(and other related references)

It's just a regular day,
not much percolating.
I hear the drip, drip, drip
of rain off the gutters,
running onto the grounds.
I have a latte pent up energy,
so I need to espresso myself
before I go to pot.
Recently I sanka lot of money
into going to Australia.
I asked a friend,
Would you like to go
for a coffee, Mate?
It was so hot
I almost roasted.
I told myself
You need to Folger tent
and go home, where you
are the cream in the cuppa.
It was just a decafe day.

False Alarm

Blond beauty saunters
near el fresco diners,
tosses long curly hair.
Thick black lashes
sweep rosy-red cheeks.
A smile curves pouty lips.

An eighteen-carat pendant
swings over perky breasts.
A short fuchsia dress
clings to slim waist and hips.
Gold-tone stilettos
tap, tap, tap the sidewalk,

draw the attention of men
whose eyes stray sideways.
They dare not turn their heads,
as their wives, green with envy
size up the competition.

Strutting around the corner,
synthetic hair smoothed,
fuchsia dress adjusted,
he hurries to the stage door.
A black on white sign announces:
"La Cage a Faux-Auditions."

A Touch of...

It's funny how forever goes so fast
and the present quickly turns into the past

It's funny you can laugh until you cry
and white is the color of a lie

It's funny dark can be so bright
and good night doesn't mean goodnight

It's funny that a poem can have no rhyme
and a day can feel like the end of time

It's funny you can love and also hate
and you can cause a twist of fate

It's funny life's filled with irony
yet it doesn't seem funny at all to me

Ladybugs for Lexi

I wish you a "Lexi" cake
with seven candles
ice cream cones
pounds of presents
and tons of friends.

I wish you ladybug luck
puppy dog licks
kitty cat cuddles
and tea for you
me and Emily.

I wish you Grandpa-
Grandma hugs
Mommy-Tony kisses
after your candles
are blown out...

I wish you
a hop-scotch spring
a somersault summer
a happy birthday
and lots of ladybug love!

Tribulation

The Dirtmen of the Apocalypse ride in,
chase dust bunnies under the bed.
The cleansing battle begins.

She runs to her storeroom,
bows before her Trinity
of Borax, Clorox and Windex.

With aerosols of mess destruction
she waxes nostalgic over her
lavish possessions.

The Duncan Phyfe is dusty,
her Baroque needs burnishing.
Upset, she flings her Ming,

polishes off the Dirtmen,
rebuffing their Pledge to return.
Dust to dust.

Go For the Gold

I call for you,
you don't hear me.
That's what you get
for ignoring me
for hundreds of miles
across five states,
tucked in a suitcase
in the trunk of
a stuffy rental car.

When we retire
to hot motel rooms,
you never bother
to take me out
unless you want
to show me off.

You search in vain
in the same places,
never thinking
inside the box.
When you accept
that I am lost,
it doesn't take long
to replace me,
Mrs. heart of stone.

You finally admit
that you miss me,
confess my successor
is not the real thing.
When I think you've
suffered long enough,
I give you a ring.
Maybe next trip you
will be more careful,
now that you realize
I am solid gold.
So here I am
where I belong,
wrapped around
your two-timing finger.

Is it true that in time we two will look alike?
If so, I hope I get your nose.

~ Marilyn L. Kish Mason

Who Said?

Who said the golden years are gold?

I was much too trusting,

my golden years are rusting,

don't believe everything you're told.

Who said the best is yet to be?

My smile turned upside-down

when I gained too many pounds,

life's best things are mocking me.

Who said you're as old as you feel?

I must be ninety-nine today,

my mind has slowly gone astray.

Golden years…what's the deal?

This Old House

I've occupied this house
for over thirty years
watched it built
from the ground up
it feels like a used house
with memories
we did not make
it's joints creak and groan
like arthritic old men

Was this craggy hill
a sacred burial ground
where arrowheads were
carved of stone and bone
soil shaped into rows
of identical dwellings

Can ghosts wait
for a house
to inhale its first breath
take possession
after the boxes
are unpacked and
furniture arranged
At three in the morning
do their vapors float
between studs and sheet rock
while we sleep unaware
do they awake
hoping to escape
their ancient purgatory
should I say *depart*
this is my house now

Monorhyme for the Contrite

I received a fine invite
to wine and dine a socialite
who had a hearty appetite,
so with innocent delight,

I RSVP'd, "Alright."
My meager funds were finite
now I know in hind-site
she saved me from my plight.

Because I am a neophyte,
my reputation has a blight.
Due to woeful oversight,
she thinks I am a parasite.

Close Call

Cast a glance
  over my shoulder
nothing there
  I feel fright

        Sinister eyes sense
          my cautious steps
        shivers run
          down my spine

Start to run
  turn the corner
don't recognize
  this darkened street

        Reach for mace
          in my purse
        press nozzle
          it's too late

My next phantasm
  should be afraid
my aim
  is truer now

Critique

Her poem seems wise

but they criticize

need to revise

again she tries

only to despise

what they reorganize

then excise

down a size

no compromise

it wins no prize

her poem's demise!

Dead Poet

Will my poetry be read
when I'm among the dead?

Will they make sense
of my past-present tense?

Will they fret or frown
at my use of verbs or nouns?

Will works by myself
languish on a dusty shelf?

Will they quote me like bards
long buried in grave-yards?

I will have the last laugh
by rhyming on my epitaph.

Writers Block
(Blank Verse)

If poetry is dead
I probably killed it.

Inspiration

I have been a seeker
and I still am,
but I stopped
asking the books
and the stars.
I started listening
to the teaching
of my soul.

~ Rumi

Listen

Years from now
when I am gone,
and you're alone
listen then for me,

hear my whispers
in the wind,
and the waves
of the sea.

When the moon
is full and high
watch for shadows
on the wall.

Before the dawn
I'll come to you.
As you dream
you will recall

the times before
my soul took flight,
when our hearts
still beat as one.

sleep in peace
for I am just
a breath away
when day is done.

The Collector

People collect curious things,
thimbles, spoons, old toys and rings.
Assortments of dishes packed in boxes,
old stamps, rare coins, pocket watches.
They add buttons, bows, pictures galore,
their house is full, yet they buy more.

Where is the joy their possessions bring,
if they fill their lives with trivial things?

My friend boasts of no solid gold pens,
he is content gathering friends.
His worth isn't measured by what he owns,
he gives of himself, and is known
as a man of kindness and deep affection.
We are blessed to be part of his collection.

The Greatest Last Gift

If the moon had not waned that night
would you have slipped into the stars?

If life and death were not one
would you have stayed with me?

When April brings gentle rain
will you know it's my tears?

If your last gift had come on time
would it have brought such joy?

Can you see beyond, do you know
it also brings me sweet peace?

For my sister Nancy

April 1931 - October 2014

Special Delivery

Rusty meowed pitifully stuffed inside a cardboard box and placed in the minivan. His little nose and paws poked out through the closed flaps as he tried to escape. He couldn't know that we "catnapped" him for a noble purpose.

Hours went into planning this "kitty caper." We just needed to pull it off. Awkwardly we carried our hostage from the parking structure to the elevator. Fearing detection and expulsion, we sneaked through heavy metal doors on the third floor. Our accomplices were late; timing was everything.

An echo sounded down the long hallway before we spied our waiting partners. It was slow going for Dad, who was pushing Danica in a wheelchair, an IV wheeling along behind her. Receiving treatment on the Oncology Ward of The Children's Hospital in Denver, Colorado, Danica was recovering from her second operation in four months for a malignant brain tumor.

Fragile from the ravages of the operations, radiation and chemotherapy, Danica was withdrawn and had stopped eating. Her once sunny disposition deteriorated since this latest surgery. We hadn't seen her beautiful smile in days. She seemed focused on the pain and nothing comforted her; thus, we hatched our little conspiracy.

It was impossible to get permission to bring Rusty to her room, so we took matters into our own hands. Ten-year-old Danica loved animals. Rusty, a frisky yellow Tabby, was her favorite pet since he came to the family as a kitten.

Slumped in her wheelchair Danica appeared too weak to look up. Her mother took Rusty from the box and placed him on Danica's lap. For a split second, there was no reaction then pure joy spread across her pale face. Her incredible topaz eyes shined. As Rusty began to play, giggles erupted from the once silent little girl. He nestled in her bruised and swollen arms, purred and contentedly fell asleep, exhausted from his ordeal in the box.

On that day, we knew our brave little Danica still had the will to recover. She would soon return home to Rusty and her loving family. She had a long struggle ahead but for now, her grateful parents and grandmother watched the scene with misty eyes. We would fondly remember the day this tiny yellow Tabby brought hope and joy to The Children's Hospital.

Lament of the Nymph

When it is my turn
time has no meaning
I skim the razors edge
blaze fresh tracks
in virgin snow
ride frothy rivers currents

Like a fledgling sparrow
fresh from the nest
I spread my wings
over towering pines

Like Narcissus
I adore my reflection
in the still-mirrored lake
my turn to prance
before the pronged stags
watching expectantly
at the forest entrance

A rose bud
a cherry blossom
an exotic orchid
envied by lesser flowers
desiring pollination
I am natures wine
ripe for the tasting

Time pales images
the razors edge dulls
mist covers the lake
the plump grape shrivels
on the dying vine
Echo fades to a whisper
Now it is their turn

You are never too old to learn.
It is never too late to follow
your dreams...your heart.

~ Marilyn L. Kish Mason

Reluctant Guru

I am not an oracle,
although I have learned
a thing or two,
which I could bestow
on young romantics,
perhaps saving them
from years of frustration
suffered at their
own naive hands.

Would my sage advice
be dismissed as
words spouted from
an extinct dinosaur?
Have I become so jaded
that I would repress the
the electric energy
coursing through their
adolescent veins?

Would I tell them
that lovers leave,
friends may betray them,
childbirth is painful,
death is inevitable?
Bless them as they revel
in their quixotic dance.
They will comprehend
it all soon enough.

From a Safe Place

Curled in a circle surrounded by calm,
floating fearless in the eye of the storm.
Not wounded by anger, nor jaded by pride,
not yet fully identified.
Unblemished body unable to hear
sounds of tomorrow drawing near.

Primal drums rhythmically pound,
the force of life draws me down.
Anchor broken, I cry out in fright,
as I emerge to glaring light.
Unnamed, naked for the world to see,
I wonder what is to become of me?

What do they read in my future,
what gifts will they nurture?
Will I be wounded by anger or pride,
will I be fully recognized?
Lovingly, gently nudged to her breast,
content for now to feel warm and blessed.

Lilacs in Winter

Ash Wednesday I knew what
I would sacrifice for Lent.
They called it a blessing.
but I curse that cancer.
Your heart grew too weary
to carry your fragile bones.
After the funeral
we gathered at Mother's.
I sat on the picnic bench
seeking solace under an oak tree.
Nearby stood a dormant lilac bush,
which would bloom at Easter,
I imagined its familiar fragrance.
The day, cold and crisp,
light snow covering the lawn.
Below a branch of the oak tree
a vibrant aura shimmered,
surrounding the shape of a man.
For an instant our minds met,
your soul appeared to assure
me you would always be near.
Often I feel your presence
as you guide our family
with your endless loving spirit.
Our lilac bush still blooms in spring.

Remembrance

Are my memories flawless
or tainted by time,
dull as an old rusty knife
once shiny and sharp?

Are they colorful creations
embroidered with yarn,
or spun on an ancient loom
with thread dyed from berries?

They hide in the woods,
I follow crumb trails
scattered in faded footprints
from a previous journey.

Memories peek around trees
like mocking children
when they tire
of their wily games.

What is the harm in designing
new versions of the past
from fragmented remnants
of the mind? What is the cost?

Witch Creek
(Beyond the Fire)

This dark Sabbath day
a Devil wind hurls fire
weaving its way
from tree to tree
in a drunken dance
of stoked desire,
reeling toward the sea.

Scudding clouds
play unaware,
like selfish children
who refuse to share
their gifts of rain
to quench the thirsty
tendrils of flame.

Nothing will save
dying brush,
dying dreams,
family treasures
turned to dust,
pyres of grief
beyond measure.

A survivor stoops,
sifts through cinders,
tenderly scoops
a ring here
a picture there
scarred reminders
of the ferocious flare.

A vision burns
where hope abides.
A seed is planted
in soil and inside
the hearts of those
who now desire
to seek new life
beyond the fire.

Joy

Find out where joy resides, and give it a voice far beyond singing. For to miss the joy is to miss all.

~Robert Lewis Stevenson

Happy Birthday

Fingers tiny as twigs
nails nearly translucent
newborn whimpers
soft as a mewing kitten,
she turns her head
towards my voice,
knows me in some
in-the-womb way.
I kiss pink cheeks
miniature nose
plumb wrinkled toes,
know her in some
in-the-womb way.
She will never be
this young again,
for this moment
I want her to be,
smell that pure
sweet baby scent,
feel love so deep
it shocks the heart
into a new rhythm,
the startling pulse
of a mother's love.

Ode to a Poet's Daughter

You are my poetry
my perfect artistry
my bright new creation
I didn't dream of you
in anxious desperation.
You are a blessing
my reason for rhyming
with lucid intention.

No lover's fascination
no dramatic disillusion
or writer's blocked confusion
only clarity and inspiration...
a verse written from the start
on the pages of my heart.
You are my cherished pearl,
beautiful beloved girl.

Here in My Heart
(Adoption)

You lived in my heart
long before you were born,
a dream waiting to come true.
My wish on a star
from the top of a mountain,
all my candles blown out,
coins tossed in a fountain,
I was here hoping for you.

I prayed for a miracle
for so many years,
searching for a clue
to my fairy tale ending,
patiently waiting,
always believing,
feeling you near,
I was here waiting for you.

Then God in His wisdom
smiled down from above,
and out of the blue
He delivered you here,
this precious gift He chose.
My heart overflows
with so much love,
I am here holding you.

Together we laugh,
alone we smile...
remembering why

~ Marilyn L. Kish Mason

Day Glow

I arise from the dark hours,
turn on my internal switch,
bask in an Eastern blush
that casts slanted rays
on my bedroom wall.

A lone Mourning Dove
coo's her soft lament.
Shrubs beneath my window,
full of spring's pink profusion,
come alive with the drone of bees.

Energized by lush signs of life
I delight in my *Ode to Joy* day,
where even the humdrum
is punctuated with tinges
of purple, yellow and green.

Each glorious scene delights
my awakened senses to savor
these moments on stormy days.
Today is my gift,
 I untie the golden bow.

Touch of Magic

A charm of humming birds
dips beaks, sips nectar
through folded tongues.

I watch in wonder
as whirling wings
dart, then hover.

Incandescent sapphire
flashes like lightening,
light up the light.

A ruby throated beauty
flickers near my cheek,
creates air upon air.

Winter winds
signal migration.
One day I will follow.

If you feel the flutter
of wings on your face
think of me as I fly away.

Welcome to Paris...

words I hunger to hear,
city of my fantasy where
I wander down vibrant streets
lined with flower-merchant carts.
Seduced by a dark, handsome
Frenchman at a sidewalk café,
he takes me to his apartment,
utters sensuous sounds of lust.
We tour the Louvre on rainy days,
where Mona Lisa looks askance
at every corner of the room.
Arm-in-arm we stroll
over the Seine, attach a padlock
to the bridge, declare undying love.

My son is a commercial pilot,
Paris is often on his itinerary.
He regales me with images;
sipping vino in pizzerias
shared with a red-haired,
brown-eyed femme fatale.
They mount a yellow Vespa,
wind their way up narrow
cobblestone streets to view
the city of crystal lights,
stop at a cabaret, hear throaty
jazz sung by a popular chanteuse
accompanied by a concertina.

He sends me gifts; a variegated
blue fluted vase purchased
at a quaint shop by the Eiffel Tower,
amber quartz necklace and earrings,
or did they come from Budapest?
J' Adore perfume from a boutique,
matching pictures made of natural
stones set in gold gilded frames,
or were they from New Delhi?
He acquires an original oil
from a street vendor hawking
art near the Moulin Rouge.

Though Paris is my fantasy
I explore a larger world
through his curious eyes.

Tierra del Encanto

Traveling through New Mexico, mercury rising to triple digits, white thunderheads plumed over the mountains on either side of the highway. The race was on to beat the storm to Albuquerque. The sky opened up just as the hotel appeared. Hard rain pelted the windows in the room and lightning came closer with each strike. Thunder caused windowpanes to rattle. Hunger drove us from our refuge to a nearby buffet. Three hours passed with no let up in the fury. Braving the storm, we ventured out to purchase fuel for our early morning departure. Under the canopy of the gas station, we could smell ozone, and feared that lightening might strike the metal roof.

As we observed the storm from our shelter a double rainbow appeared, like a bridge across the sky. The arc was complete from horizon to horizon. Between the two arcs was a wide band of darkness, lightening strikes cutting through the center. In the middle of the inner arc, gray clouds swirled and traces of sunlight glowed on their undersides. These rainbows continued for thirty minutes, vivid and mystical in desert heat until the hues began to fade;

Red; Color of energy, enthusiasm and passion, the color of the longest wavelength, a symbol of vibrancy and security. Orange; Symbol of energy and wisdom. Yellow; Brings proper clarity of thought, wisdom, and improves decision-making skills. Green; Center of the spectrum, symbol of harmony, balance, growth and good health. Blue; Color of divinity; it helps to soothe and relax. Indigo; Infinity, symbol of wisdom, intuition and self-mastery, the bridge between the finite and the infinite. Violet; Completion and the beginning of energy vibration. Flip those colors, red facing red, and that is a double rainbow.

Nature blessed us with a little bit of heaven in this scene we happened upon one hot August evening in Albuquerque, New Mexico. "Tierra del Encanto"; Land of Enchantment.

Nature

Nature does not hurry, yet everything is accomplished
~Lao Tzu

The River James

Sometimes I long to
go back to the river,
the river of my youth,
where near the shore
a tadpole army darts.
I long to thread worms
on a crooked hook
of an old cane pole,
wait for the cork to bob,
as a bullhead nibbles
at his last meal.

I long to see again,
water like a distorted
mirror reflecting saplings
on the opposite shore,
turtles perched on rocks,
heads in their shells
waiting to snap
at a finger or toe.
I envision a log
floating downstream,
instead, a brown snake
slithers in the current.

I've heard it said that
you can't go back to
the same river twice.

The tadpoles have
morphed into frogs,
oak trees still stand
on these eroded banks,
some have drifted away,
only the mighty stay.
Every moment I live
can't be the same.
As time goes by,
memories will fade,
some will remain,
but the river flows on.

Into the Woods

A songbird

tries to fly

on a broken wing

to the familial tree.

His mournful mate sings

her final rhapsody,

hovers near him

as he turns toward

those lovely deep,

dark woods,

where promises

forever sleep.

A tempest forms

too near the earth,

and as the sky falls

she weeps.

A Sprinkling of Snow

The sun submits to clouds
pushed across the sky
by chilly Northern winds.
Powder sifts onto rooftops
and lightly covers
the dun colored earth.
White new beginnings
everywhere, sparkling,
blinding the eyes.
The nuisance of winter
is patient, waits to startle,
to chill the bones.
The dusting passes,
replaced by snow banks
rising to meet the heavens.

echoes of seashells
bring the ocean
into my soul

~ Marilyn L. Kish Mason

Remember that blizzard in Boston...

snow piled over car tops,
stranded for five days,
cabin fever setting in?
An unexpected meeting
summoned you to California.
Transported to paradise,
or so it seemed,
to Carmel-by-the-Sea
near Monterey Bay,
we stay for seven sunny days
in a private cabin warmed
by a glowing fireplace,
which diminished the chill
of night sea breezes.
Looking toward the Pacific,
whales and porpoise gamboled
in frothy foam, which billowed,
licked the shoreline, withdrew
to form another wave.
Romantic walks on warm sand
revealed seashells that became
souvenirs' to remind us of
this magical place when
reluctantly we fly back
into the winter storm.

Monarch Dreams

My paper's wounded, as is my pen
my cautious start can't find an end.
Words with obscure faces
elude my vapid mind's embraces.
If my creator's timely kiss
frees me from my chrysalis,
my stained glass wings can fly,
beautify the sun soaked sky
land on yellow milkweed flowers
sow seeds among the leafy bowers.
While bees hum their symphony
my unveiled eyes at last can see
vibrant hues that still the breath,
live on despite my ordained death.
Now no longer in despair,
draw in brilliant morning air,
healing scars with my pen
I begin to write again.

Winter Checkmate

Winter came charging
on a snow-white horse,
      wind at his flank
           and icicles drawn.

He ruffled the feathers
of shivering rooks, who
      cower in hedgerows,
           chilled to the bone.

King sent his knights
to storm the keep,
      Fall surrendered
           in the dreary dawn.

A windmill, defenseless,
to it's dismay
      stood frozen in place
           and all alone.

King conquered the land
with fury and force,
      winter had won,
           earth was his pawn.

King ruled for a season
over village and farm,
      until Spring Queen checked
           and claimed her throne.

Reflections

There are two ways of spreading light: to be the candle or the mirror that reflects it. ~ Edith Wharton

Lesson of the Poet

I ignore the bouquet
of line-dried linens,
dismiss melodious
voices of spring,
deny summer flowers,
lick snow white icing
from winter's cake.
Willfully I languish
in velvet fall colors
until the chill of names
on granite markers
transcend my
egocentric self.
Tributes to lives,
carved in stone
are reminders
of my immortality.
My mind takes note,
the poetry of life
lives forever,
the labyrinth of love
is worth a fervent look
up to blue firmament
where my reborn soul
will soon take flight into
that phosphorescent night.

Ashton Inn

The ghost cannot find
the inn he once owned.
All of his old haunts are gone.
He recalls riding his Roan
down dusty main street,
hitching his horse to a saloon post.

Men inside wore bibbed overalls
drank whisky, played poker,
measured their wealth in
the growth of crops
shearing of sheep
the price of beef.

Women in bonnets walked
bare wooden boards to buy
flour at the general store.
They crafted the empty sacks
into towels, curtains, rag rugs
to adorn their dreary kitchens.

A rusty water tower now stands guard
like a centenarian sentinel. The tower
dry as the dying town beneath it.
Monolithic grain elevators
sit empty near railroad tracks,
their time of harvest past.

A new red-with-white-trim fire hall
looks anachronistic juxtaposed
with a few dilapidated structures,
siding bleached like old bones.

They lean like feeble men on crutches,
winter winds bring them to their knees.
An archeological dig will someday uncover
shards of history buried in filled-in basements
grown over with lush, green grass
nourished by the decaying flesh of the past.
The ghost hesitates, moves on,
no room in the inn...there is no inn.

Illumination

If I knew then, what I know now
I'd cross my heart and make a vow
to spend each hour as if my last,
release the chains of the past,

spend my time on joyous things,
dance as though my feet had wings,
arise to bask in morning sun,
embrace the day the earth has spun.

What I learned would set me free
to be the best that I can be.
I'd change my path in life somehow,
if I knew then, what I know now.

Mirror, Mirror

The lovely lady I envisioned
reflecting back at me,
is not the beauty I expected
she is my enemy.

Have I really met my match?
Can this facade be mine,
a distorted likeness of myself
deeply etched with lines?

Life should hold many smiles
to smooth this weary brow,
the price of life comes too high,
my mirror is laughing now.

I turn to look away,
it seems so very sad
to see how time betrayed
the truest friend I have.

By chance, a backward glance
in the out-of-focus mirror,
reveals the beauty in my heart
makes my image clear.

*The secret of a successful marriage
is to keep no secrets*
~ Marilyn L. Kish Mason

Don't Ask Me

Don't ask me to stand in your shadow,
you will block my sunlight.
Don't ask me to follow your footsteps,
I will lose my own way.
Don't carry me on your shoulders,
I won't learn to soar.
Don't kiss away my pain,
I won't learn how to mourn.
Don't help me when I fall,
I won't learn to stand.
Let me walk beside you,
be your equal,
learn from you,
teach you.
Let me share my secrets,
trust your words,
hear your regrets.
Teach me how to live
with you, or without you,
to love you without end.

Migraine

Shadowy silence breaches
the brains barrier
tossed thoughts
vanish into a vortex

Lightening in jagged lines
create painful chaos
in this constricted space
until stupor subsides

The storm passes
leaves behind relief
renewed belief in healing
a deceitful delusion

Third Child

I'd love to soar
like a fledgling dove.
Pressed to earth I fear
your frosty eyes.
You despise my friends,
my clothes, my hair.
Where were you
when I skinned a knee,
needed sympathy?

I long for laughter,
seek your hand,
you pinch my arm.
When sibling's tease
you take their side.
No bedtime stories,
goodnight hugs,
never hear *I love you*,
no lessons conveyed.

Question unanswered
as you slip away.
When I walk down
that darkened hallway,
to meet the heavenly light,
will you come to greet me
with an olive branch,
or weeping willow switch?

Alphabet Absurdity

The big A, big B, big C,
the always fatal big D,
classmates, shipmates,
workmates, soulmates,

I miss the missing-
dad gone since '76
mom gone since '84.
I'm a gray haired orphan.

More memorials,
more sad songs,
candles to light,
prayer to pray.

Mourners wearing black,
rose-covered coffins,
my fingers play
a dirge on black keys.

This morning I wake,
see signs of life.
Hope a BIG letter
won't find me tonight.

Insomnia

Two hands converge
at the top of the clock,
tossing and turning begins.
Wall-to-wall worries
muddle the mind,
eyelids refuse to meet.
Synapses leap like spastic frogs,
in a pond of half dreams,
half promises of sleep.
Downy white pillows
at the head of the bed have
too many secrets to keep.

My parched tongue
tries to cry out,
immobilized by fear
of self-made monsters
crouched in dark corners,
their victim unable to hear
Mother's soft lullaby
long faded away.
Alone, defenseless,
comes desperate hope,
praying night into day.

Alchemist's potion
works its magic
panic and pain subside.
Slumber seeps into
darkened spaces where
danger and fear reside.
When dawn spreads sunlight
through uneven shadows,
all appears to be right.

Tree Sheltered Road

I nearly passed by
the tree-sheltered road
leading to the gate of my past.
Precious years have flown
since I left home to follow
a path of my own.

At the end of this lane
loved ones wait,
my heart begins to pound.
I hear no other sound,
not a soul welcomes me
as I enter sacred grounds.

Sprays of flowers bloom
in neatly groomed rows,
by familiar names
etched in stone.
A zephyr breeze whispers
that I am no longer alone.

I kneel in the twilight,
surrounded by peace
for tomorrow is foretold;
someday I will be at rest,
at the end of this
tree sheltered road.

Romance

We loved with a love that was more than love
~Edgar Allan Poe

Good Morning

Alarm rings at five-fifteen.
Same cereal, toast, tea.
He reads the same parts
of the same morning paper.
Shave, shower, dress,
same time, same soap
same shoes, same style of shirt.
Leftovers from last night's dinner
stored in containers,
he re-heats at the office.
What is different this day,
what is special and new every day,
in every way, are the kisses.
Can't send him away
into his ordinary life
without extraordinary kisses.
No leftovers here!

Another Chapter

Dreary day done
no air
in the room
rain
pouring in

Cold dark night
no stars
blink their eyes
moon
behind clouds

Vast lonely bed
lover gone
half-empty closet
heart
turned blue

Same sad song
different day
dried rose petals
pressed
between pages

Dreamscape

He holds her hand
leads her up the stairs,
seeking solitude
in the darkened room.
Tender kisses glide her
past the silvery moon.

Her head softy nestles
on his sturdy breast.
A nocturnal bird at rest,
her hair like ruffled feathers
fanned by flowing
currents of his breath.

Her body's sloping hills
slumber into dreams
she won't recall.
Shades leaking dawn,
weave wistful patterns
on the textured wall.

Hold on to me my love,
I dreamed the wind
swept you away.
Her mind in disarray,
she reaches for his hand,
it turns into a dove.

Fait Accompli

I moved here
you moved there
    me to Sacramento
        you to San Diego

this was a lifetime
or so it seems
    and another spouse
        or two ago

where is the architect
who put this plan together
    should be time to converge
    New York chose you
        Denver chose me

finally here we are
in the same town
    in the same room
    on the same hot night
        fate finally got it right

Betrayal

He doesn't see
the meteor streaking
through darkness,
aimed at his heart.

His soul burns
from the light,
as vows shatter
into grains of sand.

Footprints erode,
then vanish,
as they drift
away with the tide.

Impossible to find
his way back home,
he utters one final cry
before their last goodbye.

We wonder, what is love?
If this is not, nothing is.

~Marilyn L. Kish Mason

Red Lion Winter

Piano man plays
in the dimly lit bar
for tips patrons toss
in a clear Mason jar.

Red door swings open,
snow enters the room
along with a vision
that lights up the gloom.

He asks her to dance
she politely declines,
heads for the phone booth
and inserts a dime.

He swallows his pride,
asks her once more,
phone call forgotten
they waltz on the floor.

They dance for hours
close up the bar,
trudge through snow
drive away in his car.

Two lonely people
begin their affair,
as he unties the ribbon
that sweeps up her hair.

Two happy people
become man and wife,
they love the Red Lion
for the rest of their life.

If Only

If you were a movie star
I'd be your biggest fan
always and forever
you'd be my leading man

If I could live forever
and you could too,
until the end of time
I'd want to be with you

If I were a song bird
and you were on the wing
I'd fly away with you
and return every spring

If I were a Sockeye salmon
and you swam away at dawn,
I'd follow you upstream
where we would go to spawn

If you were my winter
and I were your spring
I'd melt your frozen heart
and give you everything

Out of Nowhere – (A Poem)

Words tumble from my head,
miss the parchment, fall to dirt.
Fire-crackle off the page,
age the ragged edges of a Sonnet
with your smoldering embers.
Tears extinguish passion,
sizzle, pop, heat is gone.
Weeping spots the page,
restraining my quatrains
from making quantum leaps,
may as well write in the shower.
I caress my frigid pen,
hoping to ignite sparks.
Silver oxidizes
behind a clouded mirror.
Metaphors rise like butterflies
I try to catch as they flutter by.
Great news
no ink stains
on my fingers tonight.

Temperature Rising

Heat presses against
porous stucco walls,
blows through cracks
in the sultry bedroom.

An out-of-balance fan
whirs a lopsided tune
spinning the room
out of rhythm.

A mosquito circles,
buzzes a warning,
spying bare flesh,
dives in for a snack.

Protesting bodies
toss and turn
to the cadence
of intrusive noise.

Sheets spring leaks
in the muggy air,
worried and twisted
from mattress gymnastics.

Eyes avert numerals
marking minutes in
hot pursuit of slumber.
Tomorrow calls for rain.

Romancing the Rose

Among the flowers dark and fair
blooms a rose beyond compare.
Dewy tears of memories
gently fall upon her leaves,
glimmer in the morning light,
wash away each trace of blight.

Though others would do, I suppose,
one rarely finds the perfect rose,
an earthly gem so purely formed,
don't fear to reach between the thorns.
Don't wait for frosty gloom of fall
to pluck the reddest bud of all.

Sadness

Where My Books Go

All the words that I gather,
And all the words that I write,
Must spread out their wings untiring,
And never rest in their flight.
Till they come to where your sad, sad
heart is,
And sing to you in the night,
Beyond where the waters are moving,
Storm darkened or starry bright.

~ W. B. Yeats

Christmas Interrupted

(Memorial Day)

An unlit angel keeps vigil,
guarding still wrapped gifts
beneath the barren boughs.
Carolers pass a darkened door
opened days before
to unwelcome visitors
who entered the hallway
bringing in a chilly draft,
that blew out the candle
in the window.

Memorial Day winds unfurl
Old Glory as she waves
proudly in the distance.
Honor Guards stand rigid.
Glints of steel turn skyward,
salutes split the somber air.
A bugler sounds his cry,
as tears fall on trampled grass,
mingling with morning dew.

The crowd dwindles,
two fractured souls remain,
lovingly place a wreath
upon the upturned soil
before a white cross
at the end of a long row.
Words etched upon
his granite marker,
gives eternal meaning
to the inscription;
Let there be peace on earth.

The Silken Threads

Drawn to a shaft of light
she perceives an open door.
Breathing her last breaths,
sensations touch her cheeks,
then gently drift away,
delicate strands now broken
can never be rewoven.

The weaver's work
has come undone,
too late to reverse the clock,
or turn the hour glass around.
Familiar voices call her name,
she takes their hands to explore
rooms beyond the open door.

Chief Petty Officer

Duty called when
he was seventeen.
He packed his sea bag
with whites and blues,
slung it over his shoulder
and disappeared
into the Pacific
aboard the Salmon,
the Greenfish,
the Volador.

Thirteen years later
he surfaced from
periscope depth,
found himself in a
windowless cubicle
smaller than a sonar shack,
doing corporate test dives,
listening for whales...
watching for land sharks.

Century 16
(Aurora Colorado theater shooting)

May the fires of Hell burn bright
sear the serpent's sins away
may the Devil make him pay
for the evil deed he did that night

He blazed into *The Dark Knight*
his mind in moral disarray
may the fires of Hell burn bright
sear the serpent's sins away

Those who saw this deadly sight
and were caught up in the fray
know he will face his judgment day
when the truth will come to light
may the fires of Hell burn bright

Too Late

Mother, too busy,
you could have taught
me more about what
life held in store.
Dad, I am sad you didn't
have a better job,
a nicer house, newer car.
Brother, why did you poke
and provoke me?
Pretty sister, your clothes
are now my clothes.
Death leaves me with
no one to hear my pain,
no bones to pick.

Last Dance

Coifed, luminous gray hair
contrast to gray threads in her head.
At her window she smiles,
reaches upward, fingers flutter
a bird in flight.

Hearing silent music,
Swan Lake, she is the swan,
lithe, beautiful, full of life.
Her delicate dress folds
feather light around her body.

She was born to be here,
en pointe like Odette.
Floating across the stage,
Prince Siegfried lifts her
lovingly into the air

where she sees her future.
No longer a swan
she takes one last bow,
then leaps into the lake
to join her love.

Epiphany

On their twelfth anniversary
she dons her too tight
                white nuptial gown
tangled threads and shredded lace
                the seams pull apart

She leafs through their album
gazes on carefree faces
                images cracked and faded
corners dog-eared
                she closes the cover

She walks through her home
it appears unchanged
                she feels alone
the rooms in her mind
                need renovation

No way to recover
twelve pilfered years
                she realizes thirteen
is an unlucky number and
                walks out of the door

Sadness is not the opposite of joy,
together they are written
in the chapters of our life

~ Marilyn L. Kish Mason

Tremors

(Parkinson's Disease)

Plunged headfirst
into a tremulous sea,
we're tossed
by time and tide,
left to tread water,
limbs numb from
hypothermic waves.

He grows weak, weary.
No swift surgical bite
by a hungry shark-
piranhas slowly nibble
him to bare bones.
No brave sailor
will rescue us.

Poseidon dashes me
onto the rocky shore
where I lay until
the angry sea calms.
I watch for dolphins
to beckon me back
to the salty surf.

When Does Grieving Begin

With the first finger tremor
The dreaded diagnosis
Struggles to fight
depression, memory loss
Entering Hospice care
where my resolve dissolves
Placing the urn
at the funeral
When flowers fade
Clearing closets
Viewing picture albums
sleepless in a half-empty bed
After the one-year memorial
Does grieving end

Darfur

Day surrenders to night.
Greed gives rise to empires;
the weak crumble,
fortunes won;
humanity lost.

Tomorrow's promises
slumber on soiled pillows.
Morning's reality
melt assurances
of safety and peace.

Tears of infected children
slip to barren soil,
ravaged naked bodies
hunger for a chance
to realize their worth.

Wheels turn, going nowhere,
an illusion of purpose, making dust.
Helpless, they pray for answers,
but dare not pose the questions.
Pleas vanish with searing winds.

Borus Crabtree

Borus sat at church
in the very last seat
of an empty row.
He spoke to no one,
no one spoke to him...
    They didn't know what to say,
    so they turned away.

At family reunions
he folded his arms
over his concave chest,
mouth drawn tight
into a hyphen...
    He didn't know what to say,
    so he turned away.

Borus stayed late at night
buried in his work,
he never was promoted,
his boss passed him over
without a second look...
    He didn't know what to say,
    so he turned away.

Borus always somber
arriving home at night,
didn't converse at dinner,
failed to hug his children,
or compliment his wife.
    She didn't know what to say,
    so she moved away.

When Mr. Crabtree died
no friends came to mourn.
His sons sat silent by his urn.
The Preacher beseeched them
to speak a final token...
There was no more to say,
so they walked away.

Flight of a Father

She tried to wrest him
from the walls
of her heart long ago.
Like vines entwined,
too deeply rooted,
they remain linked by
the children they gifted
to the universe.
Now he lies in a hospital,
ensnared by tubes, wires,
blood refusing to flow
through occluded veins.

His children fly to his side
for their final goodbye.
She offer's comfort,
they must each reach
inside their heart
for sweet memories,
or sad regrets for things
said, or left unsaid.

His second wife left him,
his first feels only mercy.
Years ago she cast all
bitterness to the wind,
to drown in the sea,
or to melt in healing sun.
His spirit will live inside
those who love him.
His ashes set free,
his seeds remain
as he soars graceful
as his model airplanes.

Gale Winds Toss Wreckage on the Shore...

the lover's lot unknown,
the heart needs time
to catch the awareness
of the mind.

I wander by the sea,
contemplate the fate
of love not meant to be,
my heart caught up too late.

Fog, bleak and dark
will surely lift in time.
Tide sweeps away all marks,
as pain of loss subsides.

A grain of sand is fragile,
a dune stands tall and free.
Winds will change the angles,
to be what it will be.

Sliding Down the Glacier

Ouch!
I've been poked.
A rusty needle
punctures the scab
on my heart.
Wounded by words
your weapon of choice,
spitting venom
jabs the wall between us.
Cold!
I lie on frozen granite.
You stare into my eyes,
they mirror broken images
of my love.
A candle in my soul gutters.
Sliced!
with your tongue,
pierced by your look.
I hear the beat
of buzzard wings
above my bed.
I slide like air,
down the glacier,
fly toward the sun.

Bristlecone Pine

Morning dew captured
in spider webs
sparkle like gemstones
hung on silken threads.

Time ticks down
as numbers fall
to the lifeless bottom
of his internal clock.

Memories twisted,
lost in his mind,
old as Methuselah,
this Bristlecone Pine.

Shaded pathways
once lit by sun
conceal footprints faded
by harsh winter winds.

Night creatures swoop
to the forest floor,
feed on helpless
half-sleeping prey.

He is lost in this
primeval place
until looking skyward
for the only way home.

Marilyn L. Kish Mason

Born on the plains of South Dakota, Marilyn enjoys writing about prairie farm life. Her love of writing came from her father, who had a great sense of humor, and like Marilyn, was a nocturnal reader. She has traveled throughout the United States. Alaska is the last state on her "Bucket List." While living in Concord, Massachusetts she visited the homes and graves of several great writers and poets. It was there, while taking a creative writing course at Middlesex College that she was inspired to write short stories, which led to writing poetry.

After her children grew up she retired from her accounting career, and began to write again. Mary Harker and her fellow Oasis students motivated her to develop her writing skills. Marilyn's poetry appears in editions of The Oasis Journal, The International Library of Poetry, San Diego Poetry Annual, on Internet sites, and in a book authored by a friend. Stories by survivors of the Witch Creek fire in San Diego County inspired her to write about the experience.

Recently she moved from Santee, CA to Littleton, Co., giving her new fodder for her poetry...from the prairies...to the oceans...to the mountains...

Marilyn is pleased when people identify with the feelings expressed through her written words.

Marilyn Mason's poetry showcases the personal through her effective use of description, imagery, rhythm and rhyme. Passion permeates her work, draws us into each poem and keeps us there.

~Mary Harker,
    OASIS, Teacher, MFA, San Diego State University

Mason's precise yet lyrical images infuse the reader's sensibilities. Her poetry feels both highly personal and universal at the same time. I'm always happy to include her poems.

~Leila Joiner, Editor, *OASIS Journal*

Mason takes the challenges and chaos of everyday and turns them into extraordinary reflections and clever prose. There is so much knowledge and comfort between these pages. Highly recommended.

~Carol Sveilich, Author, MA
    But You LOOK Just Fine &
    JUST FINE: Unmasking Concealed
    Chronic Illness and Pain